JAN 0 8 2010

How does a
WATERFALL
become
ELECTRICITY?

Mike Graf

Raintree

Chicago, Illinois

www.heinemannraintree.com
Visit our website to find out more information about Heinemann-Raintree books.

To order:
☎ Phone 888-454-2279
💻 Visit www.heinemannraintree.com to browse our catalog and order online.

Edited by David Andrews and Laura Knowles
Designed by Richard Parker and Wagtail
Original illustrations © Capstone Global Library, LLC 2010
Illustrated by Jeff Edwards
Picture research by Mica Brancic
Originated by Modern Age Repro House Ltd
Printed and Bound in the United States
by Corporate Graphics

14 13 12 11 10
10 9 8 7 6 5 4 3 2 1

Library of Congress Cataloging-in-Publication Data
Graf, Mike.
  How does a waterfall become electricity? / Mike Graf.
    p. cm. -- (How does it happen?)
  Includes bibliographical references and index.
  ISBN 978-1-4109-3448-2 (hc) -- ISBN 978-1-4109-3456-7 (pb)
  1. Water-power--Juvenile literature. 2. Electricity--Juvenile literature. 3. Hydrodynamics--Juvenile literature. I. Title.
  TC147.G665 2008
  621.31'2134--dc22
                    2008052653

Acknowledgments

The author and publishers are grateful to the following for permission to reproduce copyright material: istockphoto **background image** (© Dean Turner); Photolibrary pp. **4** (Stefano Brozzi), **5** (Oxford Scientific (OSF)/Patricio Robles Gil), **6** (age fotostock/David Paynter), **7** (Digital Vision), **9** (The Irish Image Collection), **10** (John Warburton-Lee Photography/Julian Love), **12** (Oxford Scientific (OSF)/John Downer), **15** (Flirt Collection/Lester Lefkowitz), **17** and **22** (Corbis), **18** (Japan Travel Bureau/JTB Photo), **20** (First Light Associated Photographers/Peter Mintz), **21** (Tips Italia/Sergio Tafner Jorge), **24** (Digital Vision/Joseph Sohm/VisionsofAmerica.com), **25** (Mauritius/Herbert Kehrer), **26** (age fotostock/Peter Bowater), **27** (Robert Harding), **28** (Alaskastock/John Pezzenti Jr); Reuters p. **13**; Science Photo Library p. **8** (Sheila Terry).

Cover photograph of a cascading waterfall at Krka National Park, Sibenik-Knin, Croatia (top) reproduced with permission of Photolibrary/Digital Vision/Wilfried Krecihwost and lights and lightbulbs in Las Vegas, Nevada, USA (bottom) reproduced with permission of Rex Features/Paul Brown.

Every effort has been made to contact copyright holders of any material reproduced in this book. Any omissions will be rectified in subsequent printings if notice is given to the publisher.

All the Internet addresses (URLs) given in this book were valid at the time of going to press. However, due to the dynamic nature of the Internet, some addresses may have changed, or sites may have changed or ceased to exist since publication. While the author and Publishers regret any inconvenience this may cause readers, no responsibility for any such changes can be accepted by either the author or the Publishers.

Contents

Some words are shown in bold, **like this**. You can find out what they mean by looking in the glossary.

What Is a Waterfall?

It has been a long, stormy winter. The mountains are covered in snow.

In springtime, the snow begins to melt. One by one drops of water trickle out of the ice, creating a small stream. As more water feeds the stream, it grows and runs faster, moving downhill.

Eventually the stream runs into a large, swollen river. Soon it is tumbling and churning, bringing a powerful flow of icy water with it.

A clear, cold mountain stream becomes Skogafoss Falls in Iceland.

Skogafoss Falls, Iceland

Suddenly the ground beneath disappears. The rapidly flowing river falls freely as a beautifully arching **waterfall**. The water pounds down on the rocks far below.

A steep drop

Angel Falls in Venezuela is the world's tallest waterfall. It drops 979 meters (3,212 feet) before finally crashing onto the ground below.

Angel Falls, Venezuela

For many years, people have known about the power of falling water. They have found ways to capture this energy and turn it into **electricity**, or the power in our homes and factories.

The Power of Falling Water

Anyone who has seen **waterfalls** up close knows how powerful they can be. Water starts at the top as a gently flowing river. But, by the time it reaches the bottom, that same water seems to be an unstoppable force of tumbling and churning white water.

Victoria Falls is one of the world's most famous waterfalls.

Victoria Falls, Zimbabwe

The strength, or force, of the water is caused by **gravity**. Gravity is a force on Earth that pulls everything down toward Earth's surface. The farther the water falls, the more powerful the force.

Where does the energy of the water come from? It comes from the Sun. Warm sunlight heats the water in oceans and lakes. This energy causes the water to evaporate, or turn into a gas, and rise into the air. The energy is released when the water falls back to Earth as rain. The water continues to lose energy as it pours down mountains and over cliffs, falling down to the lowest point it can reach.

Yosemite Falls, United States

Yosemite Falls drop over 700 meters (2,300 feet) from the high mountains to the Yosemite Valley floor.

The Waterwheel

The **waterwheel** developed over time, but most waterwheels share the same basic features. Most are made of wood or metal. The wheels often have blades or buckets on them to catch the water that will turn the wheel.

As water heads toward the wheel, it is channeled through a gate. The gate helps to keep the water flowing smoothly against the wheel.

If the wheel has buckets, they fill with water on one side of the wheel. As the buckets are filled, the side with water becomes heavier. This extra weight turns the waterwheel. Waterwheels with paddles or blades are set up in fast-flowing water. For these waterwheels, the force of the water running against the paddles turns the wheel.

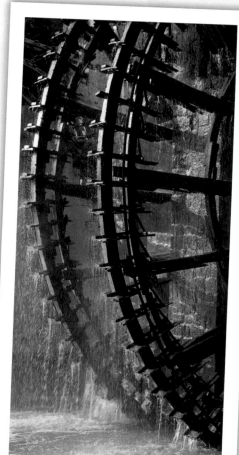

The blades of a waterwheel help the wheel to turn.

As a waterwheel turns, it also turns a **shaft** (a kind of bar) attached to the wheel. This shaft powers a machine that does the work, such as grinding grain.

This diagram shows how a waterwheel uses water power to grind grain.

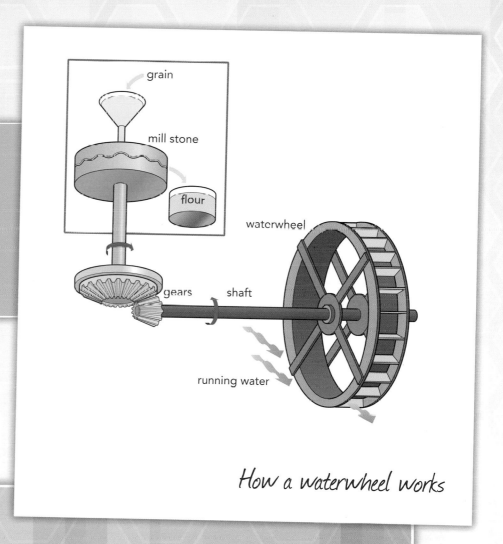

How a waterwheel works

Smoky Mountain mills

Two **mills** are still in use today in the Great Smoky Mountains National Park in North Carolina and Tennessee. People can visit the mills and purchase products made there.

Building a Dam

Waterwheels are built along a flowing river or stream. But rivers and streams are not always dependable. Sometimes they can flow heavily. Other times they can be just a trickle.

To make the flow of water steady, sometimes people create a **dam**. A dam blocks the river so that lots of water can build up. Then the water is slowly released at an even pace.

Kariba Dam was built to store water for people to use, as well as to produce **electricity**.

Kariba Hydroelectric Dam, Zimbabwe

The water that builds up behind a dam creates a human-made lake called a **reservoir**. The reservoir can be used for flood control, fishing, boating, or **irrigating** crops.

The Three Gorges Dam is part of the world's largest **hydroelectric plant**.

Three Gorges Dam, China

Three Gorges Dam

Along the Yangtze River in China is the world's largest dam. The Three Gorges Dam, completed in 2006, is the largest concrete structure in the world. The dam created a reservoir that is 660 kilometers (410 miles) long. Unfortunately, the reservoir flooded the homes of millions of residents, forcing them to move away.

It's Electric!

Today, the power of water is used to make **electricity**. A place that does this is called a **hydroelectric plant**.

Hydroelectric plants are usually built near the bottom of a **dam**. Being at a lower level helps these power stations use the force of falling water. Water held back by the dam pours steadily into the plant. The water is channeled through a pipe called a penstock. Penstocks are set up to help control the flow of water.

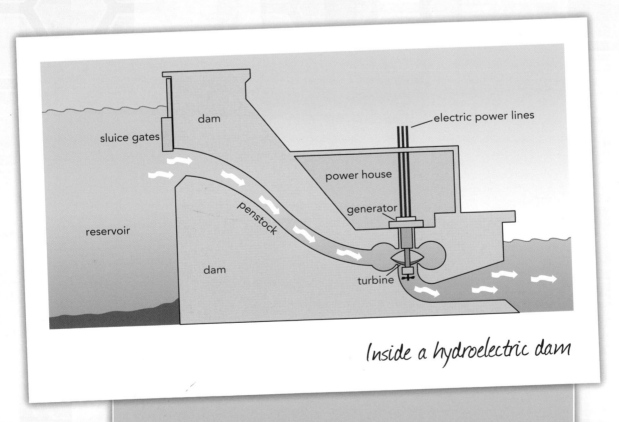

Inside a hydroelectric dam

Hydroelectric stations are located at the lower end of dams and **reservoirs** to let **gravity** increase the power of the water.

Next, the water pours over the blades of a **turbine**. The pressure of the moving water turns the blades, making them spin like a windmill. Then the turbine turns a **generator**, making electricity. Once the water passes by the turbine, it continues out of the dam and onward downstream.

Huge generators like these are found inside hydroelectric plants.

Turbine generators

A bright start

In 1882 in Appleton, Wisconsin, a **waterwheel** was set up on the Fox River. The energy from the waterwheel was used to provide light to a paper **mill**, a house, and a building nearby. This was two years after inventor Thomas Edison had created the lightbulb, so electric light was an exciting new concept. This waterwheel was the world's first hydroelectric plant.

Electricity in Our Homes

The water power that spins a **turbine** eventually becomes **electricity** that lights our homes. But how does this happen?

When water spins a turbine, it turns a **shaft** that is connected to a **generator**. The generator is what makes electricity. The round rotor, which contains magnets, spins inside the generator. Spinning magnets create electricity in the stator, a metal piece that surrounds the rotor. Wires inside the stator carry the electricity out of the generator.

Moving water makes the turbine spin. This spinning energy is turned into electrical energy in the stator.

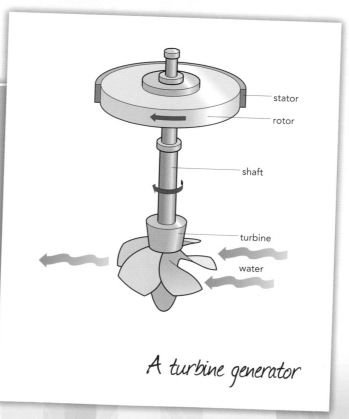

A turbine generator

stator
rotor
shaft
turbine
water

The electricity travels through the wires to a power system. From there, power lines carry it all over. The electricity is then turned into power for homes and factories.

These power lines are part of the grid system bringing electricity from plants to homes.

The biggest yet

A planned **hydroelectric** station is in the works on the Red Sea in the Middle East. When it is built it will be the world's biggest hydroelectric **plant**.

Who Uses Water Power?

Kurobe Dam is the largest dam in Japan. It is 186 meters (610 feet) high.

Kurobe Dam, Japan

The five countries that use the most **hydroelectric** power in the world are China, Canada, Brazil, the United States, and Russia. Norway, India, and Japan also get lots of electricity from water.

Canada gets more of its electricity from water than any other country. In fact, hydroelectric **plants** are so common there that many Canadians refer to any power plant as a "hydro."

What places are good for creating water power? Areas with lots of rain or snow will have more flowing water. Also, rivers that travel from high to low areas are more powerful. These are the areas where hydroelectric stations will be found.

The mountains of the Pacific Northwest in the United States are one area with both of these features. The United States gets less than 10 percent of its energy from water. Most of this comes from the Pacific Northwest.

Famous Hydroelectric Plants

Hydroelectric dams are in use all over the world. Here are a few famous ones.

Niagara Falls

This beautiful **waterfall** is on the border between the United States and Canada. Niagara Falls is a famous tourist attraction. Since 1893 some of the water has flowed through a hydroelectric **plant** instead of over the falls. It is a source of power for thousands of people.

Around 12 million tourists visit Niagara Falls every year.

Niagara Falls, Canada and the United States

Aswan High Dam

The Aswan High Dam in Egypt also uses water for power. Lake Nassar, behind the dam, is the largest human-made lake in the world. This body of water also supplies drinking water to Egypt. While doing that, it makes 10 billion kilowatts of power for the country every year.

Itaipú Dam

The Itaipú Dam in Brazil is on the Paraná River, close to the famous Iguassu Falls. It is part of the world's largest hydroelectric plant. The plant provides **electricity** to Brazil and Paraguay.

Itaipú Dam, Brazil

It took 30,000 people to build the Itaipú Dam.

A huge waterfall

There are 275 waterfalls that make up Iguassu Falls, spanning almost 3 kilometers (2 miles).

The Hoover Dam

The Hoover **Dam** in the southwest United States holds back water from the Colorado River, creating Lake Mead. This **reservoir** is the largest human-made lake in the United States.

It took less than five years to build the Hoover Dam.

Hoover Dam, United States

The dam, named after President Herbert Hoover, was built in the 1930s. It is an arch-**gravity** dam. This special type of dam curves out into the water, pushing the water to either side. The water on the sides presses on the sides of the dam, helping to hold it together.

A huge structure

When it was first completed, the Hoover Dam was the largest electrical station in the world and the world's largest concrete structure. It is 221 meters (726 feet) tall and 201 meters (660 feet) thick.

The Hoover Dam has a **hydroelectric** station. There are 17 electrical **generators** on site to create **electricity**. When the station is at full power, it can create enough power for 750,000 people! It is the 35th-largest hydroelectric station in the world.

Other Types of Energy

Water power is not the only way to create **electricity**. Here are a few others.

Fossil fuels

Fossil fuels are found in the top layer of Earth, called the crust. These are made up of the remains of tiny plants and animals. Fossil fuels, such as coal, oil, and gas, can be burned for power. Most of the world's energy comes from these fuels.

Solar energy

People can collect energy from the Sun and convert it to power. Because there is always sunlight, solar energy is renewable, or capable of being replaced by nature. The Sun's rays can be converted to **solar power** for devices that heat water, provide lighting, and more.

Solar energy plant

Power from the Sun is an alternative to burning fossil fuels.

Nuclear power plant

Nuclear power is another way to get electricity without using oil, gas, or coal.

Nuclear energy

Atoms are the smallest parts of an element. (An element is the most basic part of a material.) When they are split or fused together, they release energy. This energy can be used for power. **Nuclear power** makes up about 15 percent of the world's electricity.

Wind energy

Wind can be used for power. Wind **turbines** spin with the wind. These connect to a **generator** that produces electricity. Large wind farms have turbines set up in breezy areas. **Wind power** right now makes up 1 percent of the world's electricity.

The Benefits of Water Power

The world is running out of **fossil fuels** such as coal, oil, and gas. These fuels take millions of years to form. When we use them up, they will be gone forever.

This oil production platform takes oil from Earth's crust under the sea.

Water, however, is always with us. The water that is used to create energy goes back into oceans or lakes. It can one day be used again.

A water **plant** lasts longer than a coal plant, so people can use it longer. Water power also uses fewer workers, making it cheaper to run.

Water is a clean, clear, and constantly renewable source of power.

Water power is also cleaner than many other fuels. Burning fossil fuels causes **pollution**, meaning chemicals get into the air, soil, and water. It also contributes to global warming, or the heating of the planet. **Nuclear power** leaves behind toxic (poisonous) waste, which can be very hard to get rid of. This dangerous waste must be buried underground for many years.

Hydroelectric power, however, is much cleaner and less dangerous. There are other benefits to hydroelectric power. A **dam** can be used to control flooding in an area that was once dangerous to live near. The **reservoirs** formed can also be used for fishing and swimming.

Water-Power Problems

Water power has its problems, however. **Hydroelectric** stations can cause harm to the animals in an area.

Salmon need free running rivers without dams to return to their birthplace to spawn.

Salmon are one type of fish affected by **reservoirs** and **dams**. Salmon must return to their original birthplace up rivers and streams to spawn, or lay eggs. Passing through **turbines** along the way can harm them. In some cases fish ladders have been built to help the salmon swim over the dams. A few dams have even been torn down so that salmon can return to spawn where they were born.

Dams change the rivers downstream from them. Floods that once deposited **sediment** or soil useful for fish living in the river no longer occur. Dams also release water from the bottom of a lake into areas downstream. The water may be colder and have less oxygen. Many fish die because of this. It also may alter the way people use the river—such as whitewater rafting.

Sometimes dams for hydroelectric power can get clogged with mud. This can make the water bad for drinking. The water must be cleaned out, which is expensive.

Although making electricity from water may not work for all regions of the world, it most likely will be used more and more often in the future.

Glossary

atom smallest part of an element (the most basic part of an object)

dam structure built to hold back and store large amounts of water

electricity energy made for powering anything from lights to appliances to factories

fossil fuel coal, oil, and gas used for energy

generator machine that makes electricity

gravity force or weight of objects due to their attraction toward the center of Earth

hydroelectric related to hydroelectricity, which is when water is used to generate electricity. Hydroelectricity is often associated with a large power station.

irrigate bring water from one area to another through channels and pipes

mill machine (or building with machines) that uses waterwheels to convert flowing water to power

nuclear power using the energy made from the splitting of atoms to create power, such as electricity

plant place where a product such as electricity is generated

pollution when human-made chemicals get into the air, soil, or water

reservoir large human-made lake created by building a dam

sediment rock, sand, and dirt that has been carried to an area by wind, water, or a glacier

shaft bar that is connected to devices that move or rotate pieces of equipment in order to do work

solar power using the energy of the Sun to create power, such as electricity

turbine device with spinning blades that powers a hydroelectric plant

waterfall steep drop in a river's or stream's course that causes the water to fall directly downward

waterwheel wheel that turns by using the force, or power, of flowing water. The energy created is used to power machines and do other work.

wind power using the energy of wind to create power, such as electricity

Find Out More

Books to read

Do you still have questions about how falling water is made into electricity? There is much more to learn about this fascinating topic. You can find out more by picking up some of these books from your local library:

Orr, Tamra. *Hydroelectric Energy (Power Up!)*. Ann Arbor, MI: Chery Lake Publishing, 2008.

Raum, Elizabeth. *Water and Geothermal Energy (Fueling the Future)*. Chicago: Heinemann Library, 2009.

Spilsbury, Louise, and Richard Spilsbury. *The Pros and Cons of Water Power (The Energy Debate)*. New York: Rosen, 2007.

Websites to explore

The history of the use of water is found on this site:
www.waterhistory.org

For a complete list of the world's best waterfalls, their location and size, go to:
www.world-waterfalls.com

To learn more about hydroelectricity, visit:
www.festivalhydro.com/learn.htm

This website for kids is all about power from water:
www.tvakids.com/electricity/hydro.htm

Index